MORE JOKES FOR WOMEN ONLY

COLLECTED AND EDITED BY
SUSAN SAVANNAH

and

SHENANDOAH PRESS

Published by
Shenandoah Press
4786 Fields-Ertel Rd., Suite 264
Cincinnati, Ohio 45249

ISBN # 0-9613311-5-1

PRINTED
IN
U.S.A.

ACKNOWLEDGMENTS

I would like to take this opportunity to thank all the men. Without them, this book would not have been possible.

As a special courtesy to all the males out there who would like to enjoy this book, I have taken the time to write it slowly, as I know most of you can't read very fast.

THANKS.....

I would really like to thank everyone who wrote to me and sent in jokes. I enjoyed your letters immensely. A special thanks to the women and men of Desert Storm who had a few of my books over there to pass the time and sent back some great jokes and greetings. We are all very proud of you.

Also thanks to my friends and acquaintances who always remember the jokes they hear, and then tell me. Especially the twisted group at Harper's Point.

I love you all.

Susan Savannah

(Here's my favorite short speech on sex:)

It gives me great pleasure.
Thank you.

While little Billy was at school one day, his mother found the boy's pet dog, Paddy, lying dead in the bushes, apparently from natural causes. She was sure that the news would be traumatic for Billy, so she tried to ease the pain by burying the dog in the backyard and erecting a marker that said: Paddy — A Good Dog.

That afternoon when Billy came home from school, his mom sat him down and said "I've got some bad news. Paddy died today." "That's interesting," Billy said non-chalantly, "Can I go up to my room and play?"

After he had been upstairs for a while, his mother decides that he is in shock and he's blocking his grief by denying the whole thing. She figures that the sooner he faces up to this, the better. She goes up to his room, where Billy is contentedly playing with his toys, and says "I built a monument over Paddy's grave. Why don't you come look at it?" "OK," says Billy, and he follows his mother outside. As soon as Billy reads the inscription, he starts sobbing uncontrollably. His mother takes him in her arms and says, "There, now, it's all right. We will all miss Paddy." "Paddy!" Billy sobs. "I thought you said 'Daddy'!"

How do you know your date suffers from premature ejaculation?

When he comes walking in the door.

What's the definition of a faithful husband?

One who's alimony checks arrive on time.

"My husband is just impossible," said Susan. "Nothing I do seems to please him. Tell me Brit, is your husband hard to please?"

"I don't know" replied Brittiny, "I've never tried."

What's the difference between worry and panic?

About twenty-eight days.

I still miss my ex-husband...

...but my aim is improving.

Three nuns went into a liquor store and asked for a bottle of bourbon.

"You sisters shouldn't be drinking hard liquor, should you?" asked the owner.

"It's not for us," said one nun. "It's for our Mother Superior's constipation."

Hours later when the owner closed the store, he saw the three nuns sitting in the parking lot, guzzling the booze like sailors. "Hey!" he said, as he walked up to them, "You told me that bourbon was for your Mother Superior's constipation." "It is," slurred the nun, "When she hears about this — she'll shit!"

My friend Marcy works at the impotency clinic.

She says it's a soft job.

What do you call a wife who moans, shudders and cries out during sex with her husband?

A hypocrite!

Three old ladies were sitting on a park bench when a flasher walked up to them and showed his equipment. The first old lady had a stroke, the second old lady had a stroke, but the third old lady's arms were too short to reach.

Doctor: (taking up his stethoscope) "Big breaths."

Patient: "Yeth, and I'm not even thixteen!"

I blame my divorce on my ex-husband's calculating mind.

He put two and two together.

A little girl was taken to the hair salon for her first time. She was scared of the new surroundings and began to cry. The hairdresser was used to children and he offered the girl a cookie. She quieted down and he began cutting her hair, but in a few minutes she started up again. "What's the matter?" he asked her. "Have you got hair on your cookie?"

"What are you, a pervert?" she snapped. "I'm only six!"

Man: Are you cheating on me?

Woman: Not really.

What is marriage?

A ceremony that turns your dreamboat into a barge.

At the girls school I attended they have very strict rules.

Lights out at ten.

Candles out at ten-thirty.

The doctor told the man he had some good news and some bad news from the test results. "I'll take the good news first." said the patient. "Your penis is going to grow two inches in length and an inch in circumference." "That's great!" said the man. "So what could be so bad?" The doctor answered, "Malignant."

*You know you're getting a little paranoid
when you put a condom on your vibrator.*

I used to be Snow White…

…but I drifted.

A little girl walked into the bathroom, saw her father in the shower, and ran to her mother screaming, "Mommy, Mommy! Daddy has a big ugly worm hanging out of his weewee!"

"That isn't a worm, Sweetheart," said her mother reassuringly. "That's part of your Daddy's body and a very important part. If your Daddy didn't have one of those, you wouldn't be here. And come to think of it.....neither would I."

*My boyfriend knows what he wants —
but he can't spell it!*

We're going to a swap meet this Saturday. We meet other couples and swap.

At the sex therapist's office, the man said his problem was that his wife never climaxed at the same time he did.

His wife was excited, he claimed, but she just couldn't let herself go and he always finished before she did. The therapist remembered one of his colleagues telling him about a similar problem and his unconventional solution.

It seems the man solved it by putting a pistol under his pillow. When he was about to climax, he pulled out the gun, fired a shot, and his wife climaxed with him.

The man said he would give it a try. Late that night the therapist got a call that his patient had been rushed to the hospital. He drove over and asked, "What happened?"

"Well," said the man, grimacing in pain, "I put a gun under the pillow, like you said. My wife was feeling frisky, so we went to bed and started making out. Just as I was about to climax, I fired the gun." "Then what happened?" asked the doctor. "She shit in my face and bit the end of my dick off!"

How can you tell if you're having a super orgasm?

Your husband wakes up.

I'm dating a banker right now and he's a great lover.

He knows there's a substantial penalty for early withdrawal.

Little Boy: Mommy, where do babies come from?

Mommy: From the stork, of course.

Little Boy: I know, but who fucks the stork?

The singles bar sleaze sauntered over to a girl standing alone and said, "Hey baby, I'd like to get in your pants." She took one look at him and said, "I don't think so. One asshole in there is enough."

I heard my ex-husband had a vasectomy.

So I sent him a bottle of Dry Sac.

I'm taking a new correspondence course in sex.

I invited the mailman in.

Why is masturbation better than inter-course?

1. *Because you know who you're dealing with.*

2. *Because you know when you've had enough.*

3. *Because you don't have to be polite afterward.*

Two good friends were talking over lunch when one said to the other, "Well, Joan, how's your sex life?"

"I'll tell you," said Joan, "my husband makes me feel like an exercise bike." "How's that?" asked her friend. "Well, he climbs on and starts pumping away," explained Joan. "But we never get anywhere."

A beggar walked up to a well dressed woman on Rodeo Drive and said, "I haven't eaten in five days."

She looked at him and said, "God, I wish I had your willpower."

What happens if you put your panties on backwards?

You get your ass chewed out.

My family is forbidden to use certain four-letter words in my house.

They include — cook, wash, dust…

A guy walks up to a girl at the bar and orders a drink. He looks her over from head to toe, and says to her, "You know, I really love to travel." The girl tries to ignore him. He puts his arm around her shoulders and says, "You know what? I also love sex. What do you say to that?" The girl turns to him and says, "You really love sex and travel?" The guy nods his head enthusiastically. "Then go take a fuckin' hike!" she yells.

*What are the three words you never want
to hear when making love?*
"Honey, I'm home!"

*There was a young man from Hong Kong,
who had a trifurcated prong.
A small one for sucking
A large one for fucking
And a **honey** for beating a gong.*

How many women with PMS does it take to change a light bulb?
One GODDAMIT!

Husband: Wanna have a quickie?

Wife: As opposed to what?

"I was in bed last night," Susan told her friend, "and my husband came home from the bar. He climbed in and started to run his hands up and down my leg. That's when I started to feel that old familiar sensation."

"Arousal?" asked her friend.

"No." Susan said, "Headache."

Why is swapping partners with your friends not such a good idea?

*It's **soooo** depressing when you get your husband back.*

My husband had a terrible accident at the golf course yesterday.

He fell off the ball-washer.

At the wedding reception, Janet and her blind date weren't getting along. Things went from bad to worse until after dinner her date secretly had a friend call him from the lobby. When the call came, he listened, looked sad, then hung up. He went over to Janet and said, "I'll have to take you home. I just learned my Grandmother died."

Janet looked up at him and said, "Thank God. If your's hadn't, mine sure would have."

Did you hear about the new combination aphrodisiac and laxative?

It's called 'Easy come, easy go.'

What does the perfect male look like?

Long, dark, and handsome.

*Right in the middle of lovemaking the husband dies of a heart attack. As the funeral arrangements are being made, the mortician informs the widow that he cannot get rid of her dead husband's hard-on and if they don't do something it will look odd in the coffin at the funeral. The widow tells the guy to cut it off and stick it up her dear departed's ass. The mortician can't believe his ears but the widow is adamant, so he does it. During the funeral, friends and relations of the dead man were concerned to see a tear in the corner of his eye, but the widow assured them that there was no cause to be alarmed. Just before the casket is closed, the widow leans in and whispers in the dead man's ear, "It **hurts** doesn't it?"*

"You know," a guy said talking to his buddies, "I'm a lucky man. I never realized how much my wife loved me until the other day when I had to stay home sick from work." "What did she do?" someone asked. "She was so happy to have me home," he said, "that everytime someone came to the door, like the mailman or the milkman, she'd shout, "My husband's home! My husband's home!"

What do coffins and condoms have in common?

They both have stiffs in them, but one's coming and one's going.

I got in trouble for going too fast in the parking lot.

I was caught doing 69 in my car.

The husband was furious when he found out the checking account was empty. When he confronted his wife, she simply said, "It's my turn." "What do you mean, your turn?" yelled the husband. "In bed," she explained, "you've been making early withdrawals for years. Now, it's my turn."

Husband: What can I do to make you more interested in sex?

Wife: Leave town.

What do female hippos say during sex?
Can I be on top this time?

What do female snails say?
Faster! Faster!

The night before her wedding, Maria talked with her mother. "Mom," she said, "I want you to teach me how to make my new husband happy." The mother took a deep breath and began, "When two people love, honor, and respect each other, love can be a very beautiful thing…"

"I know how to fuck, Mom," the bride-to-be interupted. "I want you to teach me how to make lasagna."

Definition of an orgasm:

Gland finale.

Why were men given larger brains than dogs?

So they wouldn't hump women's legs at cocktail parties.

My first husband drowned in a vat of whiskey at the distillery where he worked. Four co-workers tried to save him, but he fought them off bravely. We had him cremated and it took three days to put out the fire.

At a party a guy cornered a girl and whispered something in her ear.

"You filthy pervert!" she shrieked. "What makes you think I'd let you do a thing like that to me?"

Then her eyes narrowed and she said, "Unless you're the son-of-a-bitch that stole my diary."

I bought a doggie bra today.

It makes pointers out of setters.

I went over to this guy's apartment last night and he just assumed I was spending the night.
I got so angry, I put my dress on and left!

Amy: Can you believe I was kicked out of Disneyland just for talking to Pinocchio?

Beth: What do you mean? You had him on the ground, and you were sitting on his face asking him to tell you lies!

A woman needs only 4 animals in her life.
1. A mink on her back.
2. A jaguar in her garage.
3. A tiger in her bed.
4. And a jackass to pay for it all.

Women who want to be equal to men lack ambition.

Bob came home from work early and was surprised to find his wife stark naked in bed. "What are you doing, honey?" he asked. "Well," she said, "I have absolutely nothing to wear." "Now Sweetheart, that's ridiculous," said Bob, pulling open the closet door. "Just look in here. There's a red dress, a blue pants suit, your new blue dress, Hi, Frank, your flowered house dress…"

Do you know what my favorite sexual position is these days?
Facing Bloomingdales.

If your diaphram is a pain in the ass —

You're putting it in the wrong way!

A little girl came running into the house crying and miserable. She asked her mom for a glass of cider. "Why do you want cider?" asked Mom. "To take the pain away." sobbed the little girl. Tired of all the tears, Mom poured her a glass. The little girl immediately put her hand into the drink. "It doesn't work!" she yelled. "What do you mean?" asked Mom. "Well," sniffed the little girl, "I overheard my sister say that whenever she gets a prick in her hand, she can't wait to get it in cider."

Man: Was I your first?
Woman: What do you mean **was** I?
Have you already done it?

What do you call a sensitive actress?

Clitoris Leachman.

A college student picked up his date at her parents home. He'd scraped together every cent he had to take her to a fancy restaurant.

To his dismay, she ordered almost everything expensive on the menu. Appetizers, lobster, champagne...the works. Finally he asked her, "Does your Mother feed you like this at home?" "No," she said, "but my Mother's not looking to get laid, either."

Once upon a time King Arthur was preparing for a long campaign. Wanting to make sure the lovely Guinevere was safe from temptation, the King had her fitted with an ingenious chastity belt designed to amputate anything attempting penetration and rode off to battle.

Returning victorious six months later, the suspicious King ordered all the palace retainers to drop their pants in the courtyard. One by one, King Arthur saw stumps where their penises had been, except for one man who stood intact at the end of the line. "At least one amongst you is virtuous enough to resist temptation — a man of honor!" cried the King joyfully, throwing his arms around his loyal retainer. "And what is your name?"

The man blushed and replied, "Aaaghkohulh."

What do you do if a pit bull starts humping your leg?

Fake an orgasm.

Why do women have more trouble with hemorrhoids than men do?
Because God made man the perfect asshole.

My ex-husband went to a premature ejaculators meeting but nobody was there. He was two hours early!

Why did God give woman nipples?

To make suckers out of men.

A young couple went to the doctor's office shortly after their honeymoon complaining of exhaustion and fatigue. After the tests showed nothing, the doctor explained to them that sometimes newlyweds can wear themselves out in the first few weeks of marriage. He prescribed rest and suggested for the next month to limit their sexual activity to the days of the week that have an 'R' in them. "That's Thursday, Friday, and Saturday," said the doctor. "Follow my instruction and you'll be feeling better in no time." Since it was the end of the week, the couple had no problem following the doctor's advice, but on Sunday night the young woman was very horny and couldn't get to sleep. After tossing and turning for hours, she finally shook her husband awake. Sleepy and confused, the husband mumbled, "What's wrong? What day is it?"

"Mondray," she said.

A young woman with a baby was shown into the hospital examining room. The doctor examined the baby and then asked the woman "Is he breast fed or bottle fed?" "Breast fed," answered the woman. "Strip down to your waist," the M.D. ordered. The woman did as she was told and the doctor examined her breasts. He squeezed and pulled each one for awhile and then he sucked hard on each nipple. Suddenly he remarked, "No wonder this child is suffering from malnutrition. You don't have any milk!" "That's right," said the woman. "This is my sister's child." "Well," said the startled M.D., "I had no idea. You shouldn't have come." "I didn't," replied the woman, "till you started sucking on the second one."

I've been experimenting with a lifestyle that involves living together without sex. It's called marriage.

Researchers at John Hopkins have pinpointed the main cause of teenage pregnancy. It's called a "date."

I know a very fastidious couple.

She's fast and he's hideous.

Husband: "I saw you with a strange man today at lunch. Now I want an explanation and I want the truth!"

Wife: "Well, make up your mind. Which do you want?"

There was a young man from Shreveport
whose prick was remarkably short.
When he got into bed
the young woman said
"This isn't a prick, it's a wart!"

Jessica was toweling off in front of the mirror when she noticed a few gray pubic hairs. She bent down and said to her privates, "I know you haven't been getting much lately, but I didn't know you were so worried about it!"

Do you know how much my ex-husband used to spend on liquor a month?
A staggering amount.

My ex-husband was an M.D.

Mentally Deficient.

The couple were engaged in foreplay when the woman said, "Why don't you make my pussy talk?" "How do I do that?" asked her partner. "Put a tongue in it."

Ginger Rogers did everything Fred Astaire did...only backwards and in high heels!

As Joe got Megan into bed he told her, "Don't worry, I'll be gentle."

"I wouldn't worry about that if I were you," Megan said as she looked him over. "How much damage could you do with that?"

Four years ago my ex-husband went to what he thought was a nude beach. It turned out that it wasn't, and he was arrested for indecent exposure.

They let him go due to lack of evidence.

A little girl asked her mother "Where did I come from?" Her mom was caught off guard but thought it was probably time for this talk anyway. They sat down in the living room and the mother goes to great lengths to explain the birds and the bees. She gives a graphic description of human intercourse, creation, and right up through birth. Exhausted, she asks her daughter, "Do you understand now?"

"Not really," says her little girl. "Mandy says she came from Michigan, but you haven't told me where I came from yet."

What do you call a mushroom with a nine-inch stem?

A fun-gi to have around!

Organizers of National Orgasm Week were disappointed to learn that the majority of those polled only pretended to celebrate.

My aunt used to tell me there were three kinds of sex in a marriage. There was exciting sex, necessary sex, and hallway sex.

Exciting sex is when you're first married and you can't wait to get at each other. Necessary sex is after you've been married for seven or eight years and it's more of a chore than anything else. Hallway sex is after you've been married for thirty or forty years and you pass each other in the hallway and say **"Fuck You!"**

A little girl was out with her Grandmother when they came across a couple of dogs mating on the sidewalk. "What are they doing, Grandma?" asked the little girl. The Grandmother was embarrased, so she said, "The dog on top has hurt his paw, and the one underneath is carrying him to the doctor."

"They're just like people, aren't they Grandma?" said the little one.

"How do you mean?" asked Grandma.

"Offer someone a helping hand," said the little girl, "and they fuck you everytime!"

I was so embarrassed last week.
My Ben-Wa balls set off the metal detector at the airport.

If whiskey makes you frisky and gin makes you grin, what makes you pregnant?
Two highballs and a squirt.

For Christmas, Sonny finally got the chemistry set he had been bugging his parents for. He took it to the basement and stayed down there all day. Eventually, his dad went down and found him surrounded by test tubes, pounding something into the wall. "Why are you hammering a nail into the wall?" asked his dad. "It's not a nail," said Sonny. "It's a worm!" He showed his dad the solution that he had soaked the worm in, and his Dad said, "I'll tell you what. You give me the test tube with the solution in it and I'll buy you a Toyota." Sonny handed the test tube over. The next day when Sonny got home from school he saw a brand new Mercedes-Benz parked in the driveway. He asked his Dad about the car. "Oh," said his father, "the Toyota is in the garage. The Mercedes is from your mother."

Why is life like a penis?
Because when it's soft it's hard to beat,
but when it's hard you get screwed.

What do you call the area between the
vagina and the anus?
A chin rest.

Two whales were swimming out in the Atlantic when a whaling ship appeared ahead of them. "Hey," said the one, "those are the bastards that killed my parents! Let's sink their ship!" "How are we going to do that?" asked his mate. "Well," he said, "we'll swim underneath their ship and blow hard through our blowholes and it will capsize."

So they swam under the ship and exhaled hard and the boat keeled over, throwing the crew into the freezing ocean. "Now," said the whale, "we are going to eat everyone of those bastards!" His mate looked at the whalers thrashing around in the water and said, "Oh no. I don't mind doing blow jobs, but I'm not swallowing the sea men!"

What is it that goes in hard and stiff and comes out soft and wet?

Chewing gum.

Men — give them an inch...and they add it to their own.

A young woman called the doctor and said in a deep voice, "Doc, I think you've given me too many hormone shots." "The deep voice is a normal reaction," said the doctor. "Don't let it worry you. It will go away in a few weeks." "But I've also sprouted hair between my breasts," complained the woman. "That is a bit unusual," said the M.D. "How far does the hair go down?"

"All the way to my testicles!"

My ex-husband and I had communication problems. He would get mad because I wouldn't tell him who I was dating.

What is an ideal husband?
A guy with a five million dollar life insurance policy that dies on your wedding night!

What's the definition of relative humidity?
It's the sweat that beads up on your chest while you're screwing your husband's brother.

The ladies club was playing bridge on Saturday at a member's home. That woman's husband comes into the room and announces he's going to go golfing. "Nice seeing you ladies." he says. "How about a goodbye kiss, honey?" His wife walks over to him, unzips his pants, pulls out his penis, and plants a kiss right on the head. All the other ladies sat there too stunned to say anything. The woman calmly zips him back up, says goodbye, and sits down to play cards. After the husband is gone, one of the women says, "I just have to ask. Why do you kiss your husband goodbye on his thing?"

"Obviously," said the woman, "you've never smelled his breath!"

I used to call my sex life with my ex Trivial Pursuit.

What do you say when you guide your lover's tongue toward your clitoris?
This bud's for you!

A salesman who had completed a trip earlier than expected, left his wife a message on their answering machine. When he got home, he found his wife in bed with another man. He was a non-violent type and he went to his father-in-law and told him what happened. "I'm sure there must be an explanation," her father assured him.

The next day the father was all smiles. "I knew it! I knew there was an explanation," he said. "She forgot to check her phone messages."

Annie: I wonder how long cocks should be sucked?

Fannie: Same as short ones.

What's the fastest speed at which you can make love?

68. (At 69 you have to turn around and go the other way.)

After her husband died, the widow told her friend, "Things are sure expensive these days. Why, I've spent fifty thousand dollars of his money and I haven't even paid for the funeral." "What did you spend it on?" asked her friend. "Ten thousand for the plot and ten thousand for the casket," she said. "And thirty thousand for the stone."

Holding her hand up and showing a stunning diamond ring she said to her friend, "You don't think it's too gaudy, do you?"

There was a young man from Berlin,
whose dick was the size of a pin.
Said his girl with a laugh,
as she felt of his staff,
"This won't be much of a sin!"

I called my last boyfriend "Miller Lite."

Tasted good, but wasn't very filling.

"Do you have any batteries?" a woman asks the hardware store clerk.

"Yes, m'am." The clerk gestures with his finger. "Can you come this way?"

"If I could come that way," the woman says, "I wouldn't need the batteries."

Last Christmas I sent my ex-husband an erection set.

"Do you know," said the psychiatrist, "that the cigarette you're smoking is a phallic symbol?" "What's a phallic symbol?" asked his female patient. "Well, I'll show you," said the doctor as he unzips his pants and pulls it out.

"Oh, I understand," the woman said. "Like a dick, only smaller."

What's worse than a piano out of tune?
An organ that goes flat in the middle of the night.

My ex-husband is a real loser.

He got fired... from Amway!

The elderly couple were watching the preacher on T.V. when he shouted, "God wants to heal you! Stand up now and put your hand on the T.V. and your other hand on the afflicted part of your body and you will be healed!"

The woman rose to her feet and put one hand on the T.V. and her other on her arthritic leg. Her husband got up and did the same except he put his hand on his privates. When his wife saw him she said, "The preacher said God would heal the sick, not raise the dead!"

What's another name for JELL-O?

Kool-Aid with a hard-on.

What would you rather be, a light bulb, or a bowling ball?
It depends if you'd rather be screwed or fingered.

A woman who had been out of town all week was greeted by her little son who said, "Mommy, guess what? Yesterday I was playing in the closet in your bedroom and Daddy came into the room with the lady next door and they got undressed and they got into bed and then Daddy got on top of her and..." Mom held up her hand and said, "Not another word! Wait until your father gets home and then I want you to tell him exactly what you've just told me." The father comes home and the wife tells him she's leaving him. "But why?" croaks the husband. "Go ahead, Junior, tell Daddy just what you told me." "Well," said the little boy, "I was playing in your closet and Daddy came upstairs with the lady next door and they got undressed and they got into bed and Daddy got on top of her and they did just what you did, Mommy, with Uncle John when Daddy was away last summer!"

There's a new radio station in town. It's called WPMS. They divide the month up into two weeks of love songs, one week of blues, and one week of ragtime!

"I think my husband is fooling around," confided Big Bertha to her friend. "What did you find?" asked her friend, "Perfume? Lipstick?" "No," said Bertha, "the passenger side seatbelt was adjusted to half my size. It damn near killed me trying to put it on!"

My ex-husband abuses his new wife.

He stays married to her.

Looking at her paycheck, Rhonda said to her co-worker, "Nowadays my paycheck is like a handful of hard cock." "What do you mean?" asked her friend. "Well," she said. "It gives you a good feeling, but it seems like the more you work, the less you have to hold on to!"

The only time my ex-husband would wake up stiff was when he worked out at the gym the night before.

My ex had the worst breath in the world.
When he would go to our dentist, the dentist would take the laughing gas.

Man: "Honey, if I were disfigured, would you still love me?"

Woman: "Darling, I'll always love you."

Man: "How about if I became impotent and couldn't make love to you anymore?"

Woman: "Don't worry darling, I'll always love you."

Man: "Well, what if I lost my Vice President's job and wasn't bringing home six figures anymore?"

Woman: "Like I said, I'll always love you. But I'd really miss you, too."

I haven't been able to find a guy with the right size equipment. Either the guy is so small, I want to scream — or he's so big, I have to!

Sister Margaret died and by mistake she wound up in hell instead of heaven. She called St. Peter and told him what had happened and St. Peter said he would straighten it out. The next day, however, the good sister was still with the sinners. St. Peter received a second call from a panicky Sister Margaret. "You've got to help me!" she cried. "There's an orgy planned for first thing tomorrow morning!" St. Peter promised to correct the mistake, but the next day he forgot all about it. About noon he received another call, "Hey Pete! This is Maggie. Forget about the transfer!"

Cinderella was very happy for a while after marrying the handsome Prince, but eventually, she became bored. She started fooling around, and soon she was sleeping with everybody. Her Fairy Godmother warned her several times, but it did no good. Finally she became so upset with Cinderella, that with a wave of her wand she turned Cinderella's private parts into a pumpkin. Three days later, the Fairy Godmother checked in to see how she was getting along. She was amazed to see Cinderella looking happier than ever. "What's going on?" the Fairy Godmother asked.

"I've just met Peter Peter!" Cinderella beamed.

I wanted to earn some extra money when I was in college, so I applied for a job as a topless waitress.

They hired me... as a busboy!

What do you sit on that has four letters, beginning with the letter 'D' and ending with the letter 'K'?

A dock.

When Joann entered the confessional, the priest slid the door open and she said "Forgive me, Father, for I have sinned."

"How many times?" asked the priest.

"I don't know," muttered Joann. "For Christ's sake," she hissed, "I'm a lover — not an accountant!"

What does a French woman say when she's making love?
"Ah! C'est merveilleux!"

An Italian woman?
"Ah! Oo! Che meravigliosa!"

An American woman?
"Bobby! The ceiling needs painting!"

My waterbed is known as Lake Placid.

Or when my ex was there Lake Flacid.

My ex used to take me out on a royal evening.
Dinner at Burger King and dessert at Dairy Queen.

Crazy Sally went to her gynecologist when she got her vibrator stuck inside of her. "To remove that vibrator," said the doctor, "I'm going to have to perform a very long and delicate operation." "I don't think I can afford that," said Sally. "Could you just replace the batteries?"

A man was on a crowded elevator when he accidentally jabbed a young lady in the chest with his elbow. He liked what he felt, so he said to her, "If the rest of you is as terrific as your tits, I'd love to fuck you." Without missing a beat, she said to him, "If your dick is as hard as your elbow, come to room 348."

What's the difference between exotic and psychotic?

Exotic is when your lover is wearing a French tickler.

Psychotic is when he's wearing French toast!

There are six very important men in a woman's life. They are:

The Doctor: He says, "Take your clothes off."

The Dentist: He says, "Open wide."

The Hairdresser: He says, "Do you want it teased or blown?"

The Interior Decorator: He says, "You'll like it once it's in."

The Milkman: He says, "Do you want it in front or in back?"

The Banker: He says, "If you take it out, you'll lose interest."

What is the worst thing about being an atheist?

You have no one to talk to when your partner is eating you out.

Why is sex like air?

It's no big thing unless you aren't getting any.

An eight year old boy was walking home with a girl in his class when he said to her, "Sally, you're the first girl I ever loved." "Oh great!" she said, "If there's anything I don't need, it's another beginner."

Who enjoys sex more, the man or the woman? The woman, of course. Look at it this way. When your ear itches and you put your little finger in it and wiggle it around, what feels better — your finger or your ear?

The stewardess was telling one of the passengers that this was the first all-woman flight for that airline.

The pilot and co-pilot were women, the navigator was a woman, and all the flight attendants were female. "I think that's just great," said the passenger. "Do you think it would be all right if I went up to the cockpit and congratulated them?" "Excuse me," said the stewardess, "but we don't call it the 'cockpit' anymore."

How do you make Manischewitz wine?

Squeeze his balls.

A woman brings home a guy from a bar and tells him, "We have to hurry, my husband will be home soon."

"How soon?" asks the guy.

"Don't tell me you're gay!?" yells the woman.

A girlfriend of mine has been seeing a psychiatrist for as long as I can remember. Last summer she went to Europe and sent her shrink a postcard. It said — having a wonderful time...why?

One of my old boyfriends has never been married.

He's never found a woman who loves him as much as he does.

A woman went to her doctor for a check-up and was told she was in perfect health and had the body of a twenty-two year old. When she got home, she told her husband what the doctor said.

"What about your fat ass?" he asked.

"He didn't say anything about you," she answered.

Why did the woman insist on burying her husband twelve feet under?

Because deep down he was a good person.

All men are created equal.

Poor things.

A novice nun, who as part of her training, had to spend five years in a nunnery and she was only allowed to speak two words to the Mother Superior once a year. At the end of the first year, the Mother Superior asked her how she liked it there. "Bad food" the nun said and was dismissed. She was asked the same question at the end of her second year, to which she told Mother Superior, "Poor company!" At the end of the third year, the Mother Superior called her in and said, "Well, what do you have to say for yourself?" "I quit!" said the nun. "I'm not surprised," said the Mother Superior. "You've been here three years and all you've done is bitch, bitch, bitch!"

ATTENTION:

Do you know any good
'JOKES FOR WOMEN ONLY?'

If so, send them to:

Shenandoah Press
4786 Fields-Ertel Road
Suite 264
Cincinnati, Ohio 45249

Remember, there can be no compensation,
but your favorite jokes and stories will be
immortalized in print!

Thanks again,

Susan Savannah

ORDER
BY
MAIL
CLIP OUT COUPON.

Indicate which and how many
books you want to order.

Enclose a check or
money order payable to:

Shenandoah Press
for $6.50 per book.
(Price includes postage,
sales tax and handling.)

MAIL TO

Shenandoah Press
4786 Fields-Ertel Road
Suite 264
Cincinnati, Ohio 45249

107

COUPON

PLEASE SEND ME:

☐ JOKES FOR MEN ONLY

☐ JOKES FOR WOMEN ONLY

☐ MORE JOKES FOR WOMEN ONLY

NAME _____

ADDRESS _____

CITY _____ STATE _____ ZIP _____